Aristotle:
The Polymath Philosopher

Aristotle, one of history's most influential philosophers and polymaths, was born in 384 BC in the ancient city of Stagira, located in what is now modern-day Greece. His father, Nicomachus, was the personal physician to King Amyntas of Macedon, which provided the young Aristotle with a privileged upbringing. This early exposure to the court and the medical sciences would lay the foundation for his diverse interests and wide-ranging contributions to knowledge.

At the age of 17, after the death of his parents, Aristotle journeyed to Athens to study at the Academy, the renowned philosophical school founded by Plato. There, he became a student of Plato, and for 20 years, he immersed himself in the philosophical and intellectual milieu of the time. Under Plato's guidance, Aristotle's critical thinking skills, love of knowledge, and passion for philosophy blossomed. However, he did not hesitate to challenge some of Plato's ideas, particularly those related to his theory of forms.

In 347 BC, after Plato's death, Aristotle left Athens and embarked on an extensive period of travel and exploration. This sojourn is often referred to as his "wandering years." During his travels, he gained a wealth of knowledge in various fields, including biology, zoology, ethics, politics, and more. He conducted systematic observations and gathered data that would serve as the foundation for his groundbreaking contributions to these diverse disciplines. This empirical approach to knowledge was one of his most enduring legacies.

In 343 BC, Aristotle received a significant opportunity when he was invited by King Philip II of Macedon to become the tutor for his young son, Alexander, who would later be known as Alexander the Great. For the next several years, Aristotle educated the future conqueror in a wide range of subjects, instilling in him a passion for learning and a deep appreciation for the sciences and philosophy. Aristotle's influence on Alexander's intellectual development was profound, and it would later impact the course of history.

The Lyceum and Intellectual Legacy

Upon returning to Athens in 335 BC, Aristotle embarked on a new phase of his life. He founded the Lyceum, a school of philosophy that would rival Plato's Academy in influence and intellectual output. Unlike Plato's school, which focused on abstract concepts and ideals, the Lyceum took a more empirical and systematic approach to understanding the natural world, human ethics, and politics.

Aristotle's teaching at the Lyceum covered a wide range of subjects, and he had an insatiable curiosity for exploring the natural world. He delved into biology, classifying and studying animals, plants, and their characteristics. His work in biology, especially "Historia Animalium"

and "Parts of Animals," laid the foundation for
the field of zoology. He also made significant
contributions to botany and provided one of the
earliest classifications of animals.

In the realm of ethics and philosophy, Aristotle's
"Nicomachean Ethics" and "Eudemian Ethics" set
the stage for the development of virtue ethics.
He emphasized the importance of achieving
eudaimonia, often translated as "happiness" or
"flourishing," through the cultivation of
virtues. Aristotle's ethical framework
influenced subsequent moral philosophy
and remains highly regarded to this day.

Aristotle's exploration of politics and
governance led to his work "Politics."
In this treatise, he examined different forms
of government and proposed the concept of the
"polis" as the ideal political structure for
human society. His ideas on democracy,
oligarchy, and the importance of a middle-class
"polity" would have a profound and lasting
impact on political theory and practice.

One of Aristotle's most famous works,
"Metaphysics," delved into the nature of reality,
existence, and causality. He introduced the
concept of the "four causes," which includes the
material cause, formal cause, efficient cause,
and final cause. This framework remains
influential in the philosophy of science
and ontology.

Aristotle's influence extended beyond
philosophy and science into the world of
rhetoric, where he authored "Rhetoric," a work on
persuasive communication and argumentation.

His insights into persuasive techniques and the study of argumentation have been studied and utilized for centuries, even in the modern field of communication and rhetoric.

Aristotle's commitment to empirical observation and logical analysis set the standard for scientific inquiry for generations to come. His works served as the basis for much of the scientific and philosophical thought of the Hellenistic, Roman, and medieval periods. Scholars like Thomas Aquinas, Avicenna, and Maimonides built upon his ideas, creating a bridge between ancient philosophy and the medieval world.

Aristotle's contributions to knowledge were immense and multifaceted, making him one of the most influential figures in Western thought. His legacy endures in academia, science, ethics, politics, and more, and his works continue to be studied and admired for their depth and insight. Aristotle's profound impact on human understanding and the enduring relevance of his ideas ensure his place as one of the most significant philosophers in history.

Major Ideas and Philosophy of Aristotle

Aristotle, one of the most influential philosophers in history, made substantial contributions to a wide range of fields, including ethics, metaphysics, epistemology, politics, biology, and more. Here are some of his major ideas and philosophies:

METAPHYSICS: Aristotle's metaphysical philosophy is concerned with understanding the

fundamental nature of reality. He introduced
the concept of the "four causes" to provide a
comprehensive framework for explaining the
essence of things. These causes are the material
cause (the physical substance of an object), the
formal cause (the essential characteristics that
define it), the efficient cause (the process or
agent responsible for its existence), and the
final cause (its purpose or goal). Aristotle's
metaphysical framework encourages us to
consider the deeper meaning and purpose behind
the existence of all things, emphasizing that
everything has a natural place and function
in the world.

ETHICS AND VIRTUE THEORY: Aristotle's ethical
philosophy, known as virtue ethics, focuses on
the development of virtuous character as the
key to leading a good life. He argues that the
ultimate goal, eudaimonia (often translated as
"happiness" or "flourishing"), is achieved by
cultivating virtues such as courage, wisdom,
and justice. Virtue, in Aristotle's view, lies in
finding the mean between extremes, avoiding
both excess and deficiency. His approach to
ethics emphasizes the importance of character
development and moral excellence as a means to
living a fulfilling and morally sound life.

POLITICS: In his political philosophy, outlined
in "Politics," Aristotle explores the nature of
governance and the ideal state. He advocates for
the polis, or the city-state, as the most suitable
political structure for achieving the common
good. Aristotle categorizes various forms of
government, such as democracy, oligarchy, and

monarchy, and evaluates their strengths and weaknesses. His philosophy advocates for a balanced and moderate form of government, one that upholds justice and serves the collective well-being of its citizens.

EMPIRICAL APPROACH AND CATEGORIZATION OF THE NATURAL WORLD: Through systematic observation and classification, Aristotle made groundbreaking strides in biology and natural science. His empirical approach emphasized the significance of detailed observations and methodical categorization, departing from the more abstract and speculative methods of earlier philosophers. This approach, in turn, significantly contributed to the development of the scientific method.

In parallel, Aristotle's development of a categorization system that distinguished between substances and attributes played a foundational role in the study of ontology. This categorization system offered a structured framework for exploring the fundamental nature of existence and laid the groundwork for subsequent philosophical discussions. Aristotle's emphasis on empiricism and observation in these interconnected areas marked a pivotal shift in the philosophical landscape and left an enduring legacy for scientific inquiry and the study of reality.

LOGIC AND SYLLOGISMS: Aristotle's contributions to formal logic are fundamental to the field. He is often regarded as the "father of formal logic" for his development of syllogisms, a deductive reasoning method. In a syllogism, three propositions are presented, including a major premise, a minor premise, and a conclusion. For instance, consider the syllogism: "All birds have feathers (major premise), sparrows are birds (minor premise), therefore, sparrows have feathers (conclusion)." Aristotle's logical system, expounded in works like "Prior Analytics" and "Posterior Analytics," provides a powerful framework for systematic and rigorous reasoning. This logical method has been instrumental in shaping the field of logic itself and has significantly influenced the development of the scientific method, which relies on sound deductive reasoning for empirical investigations and discoveries.

ECONOMICS: Aristotle's economic philosophy underscores that the true purpose of economic activity should prioritize the well-being and flourishing of both individuals and the broader community. He saw economic pursuits as a means to an end - namely, to support a good and fulfilling life - rather than as an end in themselves. Aristotle recognized the advantages of private property over communal ownership, as he believed that private property ownership often encouraged responsible management and maintenance, reducing the risk of negligence that could occur in communal ownership. However, he also acknowledged that the issue with private property stemmed from certain aspects of human nature, such as the potential for excessive greed or immoderation in wealth accumulation. Aristotle's economic ideas thus highlight the delicate balance between private property rights and the ethical responsibilities of property owners in the pursuit of the common good.

THEORY OF KNOWLEDGE (EPISTEMOLOGY): Aristotle's epistemological framework divides knowledge into three fundamental categories: Episteme, Techne, and Phronesis. Episteme signifies scientific knowledge rooted in necessity and established through rigorous reasoning, exemplified by mathematical and philosophical knowledge. Techne encompasses practical expertise and skills relevant to various crafts and professions, such as those possessed by skilled artisans and professionals. Phronesis, often termed practical wisdom or prudential knowledge, pertains to the ability to make sound, morally informed judgments in complex, real-life situations.

This tripartite division in Aristotle's theory of knowledge reflects his profound understanding of the multifaceted nature of human cognition and wisdom. It emphasizes the interplay between theoretical and practical wisdom, highlighting the essential role each plays in comprehending the world and navigating the intricacies of human existence.

AESTHETICS: In his work "Poetics," Aristotle explored the fundamental elements of drama and poetry. He dissected storytelling and dramatic composition, emphasizing key components such as plot, character, and catharsis. Aristotle's ideas on aesthetics have had a profound and enduring influence on the analysis and creation of literature and theater. For example, his concept of catharsis, the emotional purging or cleansing that an audience experiences through witnessing a tragedy, has remained a central theme in discussions of the emotional impact of art.

PHILOSOPHY OF MIND AND UNITY OF SOUL:
Aristotle's inquiries into the philosophy
of mind were deeply rooted in his exploration
of the unity of the soul. In his pursuit to
understand the nature of consciousness, he made
a distinctive distinction between the rational
and irrational aspects of the soul, examining
the multifaceted faculties of the human mind.
One of his most significant contributions was
his exploration of the intricate relationship
between the body and the soul. Aristotle posited
that the soul is not a separate, dualistic entity
but rather the form of the body, intimately
interconnected with it. This perspective
contrasted with later philosophers like
Descartes, who embraced mind-body dualism.
Aristotle's ideas on the soul's operations and its
inseparable connection to the physical world
significantly influenced subsequent
philosophers and became foundational to the
study of the philosophy of mind and the field
of psychology.

Aristotle's multifaceted wisdom has left an
enduring imprint on human thought, spanning
across metaphysics, ethics, politics, science,
and aesthetics. His ideas continue to inspire and
challenge scholars, offering profound insights
into the fundamental aspects of life. This book
is a journey into Aristotle's mind through a
collection of his most essential quotes.
These timeless words provide a glimpse into the
philosopher's enduring wisdom, resonating with
the eternal quest for knowledge, virtue,
and the essence of existence.

Virtue is more
clearly shown in the
performance of fine
actions than in the
non-performance
of base ones.

Happiness itself is sufficient excuse. Beautiful things are right and true; so beautiful actions are those pleasing to the gods. Wise men have an inward sense of what is beautiful, and the highest wisdom is to trust this intuition and be guided by it. The answer to the last appeal of what is right lies within a man's own breast. Trust thyself.

Greatness of spirit
is accompanied by
simplicity and
sincerity.

Freedom is
obedience to
self-formulated
rules.

Anybody can become
angry - that is easy,
but to be angry with the
right person and to the
right degree and at the
right time and for the
right purpose, and in
the right way - that is
not within everybody's
power and is not easy.

While both [Plato and truth] are dear, piety requires us to honor truth above our friends.

The tyrant, who in order to hold his power, suppresses every superiority, does away with good men, forbids education and light, controls every movement of the citizens and, keeping them under a perpetual servitude, wants them to grow accustomed to baseness and cowardice, has his spies everywhere to listen to what is said in the meetings, and spreads dissension and calumny among the citizens and impoverishes them, is obliged to make war in order to keep his subjects occupied and impose on them permanent need of a chief.

The man who is truly
good and wise will bear
with dignity whatever
fortune sends, and will
always make the best of
his circumstances.

It is the mark of an
educated person to
search for the same
kind of clarity in
each topic to the
extent that the
nature of the
subject admits.

Even if you must have regard to wealth, in order to secure leisure, yet it is surely a bad thing that the greatest offices, such as those of kings and generals, should be bought. The law which allows this abuse makes wealth of more account than virtue, and the whole state becomes avaricious.

The investigation of the truth is in one way hard, in another easy. An indication of this is found in the fact that no one is able to attain the truth adequately, while, on the other hand, no one fails entirely, but everyone says something true about the nature of all things, and while individually they contribute little or nothing to the truth, by the union of all a considerable amount is amassed.

Great and frequent
reverses can crush and
mar our bliss both by the
pain they cause and by
the hindrance they offer
to many activities. Yet
nevertheless even in
adversity nobility
shines through, when a
man endures repeated and
severe misfortune with
patience, not owing to
insensibility but
from generosity and
greatness of soul.

Suppose, then, that
all men were sick or
deranged, save one or
two of them who were
healthy and of right
mind. It would then
be the latter two who
would be thought to
be sick and deranged
and the former not!

Why is it that all men
who are outstanding
in philosophy, poetry
or the arts are
melancholic?

It is of the nature
of desire not to be
satisfied, and most
men live only for the
gratification of it.

Yes the truth is that
men's ambition and
their desire to make
money are among the
most frequent causes
of deliberate acts of
injustice.

The arousing of
prejudice, pity, anger,
and similar emotions
has nothing to do with
the essential facts, but
is merely a personal
appeal to the man who
is judging the case.

Some vices miss what
is right because they
are deficient, others
because they are
excessive, in feelings
or in actions, while
virtue finds and
chooses the mean.

It belongs to small-mindedness to be unable to bear either honor or dishonor, either good fortune or bad, but to be filled with conceit when honored and puffed up by trifling good fortune, and to be unable to bear even the smallest dishonor and to deem any chance failure a great misfortune, and to be distressed and annoyed at everything. Moreover the small-minded man is the sort of person to call all slights an insult and dishonor, even those that are due to ignorance or forgetfulness. Small-mindedness is accompanied by pettiness, querulousness, pessimism and self-abasement.

The high-minded
man does not bear
grudges, for it is not
the mark of a great
soul to remember
injuries, but to
forget them.

Every action must be
due to one or other of
seven causes: chance,
nature, compulsion,
habit, reasoning,
anger, or appetite.

Bravery is a mean state
concerned with things
that inspire confidence
and with things fearful...
and leading us to choose
danger and to face it,
either because to do so is
noble, or because not to do
so is base. But to court
death as an escape from
poverty, or from love, or
from some grievous pain,
is no proof of bravery,
but rather of cowardice.

The young have exalted
notions, because they have not
been humbled by life or learned
its necessary limitations;
moreover, their hopeful
disposition makes them think
themselves equal to great
things—and that means having
exalted notions. They would
always rather do noble deeds
than useful ones: Their lives
are regulated more by moral
feeling than by reasoning....
All their mistakes are in the
direction of doing things
excessively and vehemently.
They overdo everything; they
love too much, hate too much,
and the same with everything
else.

It is best to rise
from life as from
a banquet, neither
thirsty nor drunken.

I say that habit's
but a long practice,
friend, and this
becomes men's nature
in the end.

There is a sort of
education in which
parents should train
their sons, not as being
useful or necessary,
but because it is
liberal or noble.

We must not listen to those who advise us 'being men to think human thoughts, and being mortal to think mortal thoughts' but must put on immortality as much as possible and strain every nerve to live according to that best part of us, which, being small in bulk, yet much more in its power and honour surpasses all else.

There is nothing grand or
noble in having the use
of a slave, in so far as he is a
slave; or in issuing commands
about necessary things. But it
is an error to suppose that
every sort of rule is despotic
like that of a master over
slaves, for there is as great a
difference between the rule
over freemen and the rule
over slaves as there is
between slavery by nature
and freedom by nature..

The life of money-making
is one undertaken under
compulsion, and wealth
is evidently not the good
we are seeking; for it is
merely useful and for the
sake of something else.

Politicians also
have no leisure,
because they are
always aiming at
something beyond
political life
itself, power and
glory, or happiness.

There is also a
doubt as to what is
to be the supreme
power in the state: -
Is it the multitude?
Or the wealthy?
Or the good?
Or the one
best man?
Or a tyrant?

The legislator should direct his attention above all to the education of youth; for the neglect of education does harm to the constitution. The citizen should be molded to suit the form of government under which he lives.
For each government has a peculiar character which originally formed and which continues to preserve it. The character of democracy creates democracy, and the character of oligarchy creates oligarchy.

The trade of the petty
usurer is hated with
most reason: it makes a
profit from currency
itself, instead of making
it from the process which
currency was meant to
serve. Their common
characteristic is
obviously their
sordid avarice.

We should venture on
the study of every
kind of animal without
distaste; for each and
all will reveal to us
something natural and
something beautiful.

Wishing to be
friends is quick
work, but friendship
is a slow-ripening
fruit.

God and nature
create nothing that
has not its use.

Different men seek
after happiness in
different ways and by
different means, and
so make for themselves
different modes of
life and forms of
government.

The end of this
science [ethics]
is not knowledge
but action.

Saying the words
that come from
knowledge
is no sign
of having it.

For some identify
happiness with virtue,
some with practical
wisdom, others with a kind
of philosophic wisdom,
others with these, or one
of these, accompanied by
pleasure or not without
pleasure; while others
include also external
prosperity. Now ... it is
not probable that these
should be entirely
mistaken, but rather that
they should be right in at
least some one respect or
even in most respects.

It is impossible,
or not easy, to
alter by argument
what has long been
absorbed by habit.

A brave man
is clear in his
discourse, and
keeps close to
truth.

Nature proceeds little
by little from things
lifeless to animal life
in such a way that it is
impossible to determine
the exact line of
demarcation, nor on
which side thereof an
intermediate form
should lie.

If purpose, then, is inherent in art, so is it in Nature also. The best illustration is the case of a man being his own physician, for Nature is like that— agent and patient at once.

The essential nature
(concerning the soul)
cannot be corporeal,
yet it is also clear
that this soul is
present in a particular
bodily part, and this
one of the parts having
control over the rest
(heart).

Friends are much
better tried
in bad fortune
than in good.

Love is composed
of a single soul
inhabiting two
bodies.

Everybody loves a
thing more if it has
cost him trouble: for
instance those who
have made money love
money more than
those who have
inherited it.

Suffering becomes
beautiful when any one
bears great calamities
with cheerfulness, not
through insensibility,
but through greatness
of mind.

When there is no
middle class, and the
poor greatly exceed
in number, troubles
arise, and the state
soon comes to an end.

But the virtues we get by
first exercising them, as
also happens in the case of
the arts as well. Whatever
we learn to do, we learn by
actually doing it; men come
to be builders, for instance,
by building, and harp
players by playing the harp.
In the same way, by doing
just acts we come to be just;
by doing self-controlled
acts, we come to be self-
controlled ; and by doing
brave acts, we become brave.

He is courageous who
endures and fears the
right thing, for the
right motive, in the
right way and at the
right times.

.... In a word, acts of any kind produce habits or characters of the same kind. Hence we ought to make sure that our acts are of a certain kind; for the resulting character varies as they vary.
It makes no small difference, therefore, whether a man be trained in his youth up in this way or that, but a great difference, or rather all the difference.

Poverty is the parent
of revolution
and crime.

Without friends no
one would choose to
live, though he had
all other goods.

Happiness, whether consisting in pleasure or virtue, or both, is more often found with those who are highly cultivated in their minds and in their character, and have only a moderate share of external goods, than among those who possess external goods to a useless extent but are deficient in higher qualities.

I count him braver who
overcomes his desires
than him who conquers
his enemies; for the
hardest victory is
over self.

The beauty of the soul
shines out when a man
bears with composure
one heavy mischance
after another, not
because he does not
feel them, but because
he is a man of high
and heroic temper.

The prudent man aspires
not to pleasure, but to
the absence of pain.

To unlearn
is as hard as
to learn.

But what then do we mean by the good? It is surely not like the things that only chance to have the same name. Are goods one, then, by being derived from one good or by all contributing to one good, or are they rather one by analogy?

In all well-attempered
governments there is
nothing which should
be more jealously
maintained than the
spirit of obedience to
law, more especially
in small matters; for
transgression creeps in
unperceived and at last
ruins the state, just as
the constant recurrence
of small expenses in
time eats up a fortune.

Of ill-temper there are three kinds: irascibility, bitterness, sullenness. It belongs to the ill-tempered man to be unable to bear either small slights or defeats but to be given to retaliation and revenge, and easily moved to anger by any chance deed or word. Ill-temper is accompanied by excitability of character, instability, bitter speech, and liability to take offense at trifles and to feel these feelings quickly and on slight occasions.

After these matters we ought perhaps next to discuss pleasure. For it is thought to be most intimately connected with our human nature, which is the reason why in educating the young we steer them by the rudders of pleasure and pain; it is thought, too, that to enjoy the things we ought and to hate the things we ought has the greatest bearing on virtue of character. For these things extend right through life, with a weight and power of their own in respect both to virtue and to the happy life, since men choose what is pleasant and avoid what is painful; and such things, it will be thought, we should least of all omit to discuss, especially since they admit of much dispute.

Whereas young people become accomplished in geometry and mathematics, and wise within these limits, prudent young people do not seem to be found. The reason is that prudence is concerned with particulars as well as universals, and particulars become known from experience, but a young person lacks experience, since some length of time is needed to produce it.

It concerns us to
know the purposes we
seek in life, for then,
like archers aiming
at a definite mark, we
shall be more likely
to attain what we
want.

Poetry demands a man
with a special gift
for it, or else one
with a touch of
madness in him.

Men must be able to engage in business and go to war, but leisure and peace are better; they must do what is necessary and indeed what is useful, but what is honorable is better. On such principles children and persons of every age which requires education should be trained.

But is it just then
that the few and the
wealthy should be the
rulers? And what if
they, in like manner,
rob and plunder the
people, - is this just?

Every art and every
investigation, and
likewise every
practical pursuit or
undertaking, seems to
aim at some good: hence
it has been well said
that the good is that at
which all things aim.

Nature herself, as has been often said, requires that we should be able, not only to work well, but to use leisure well; for, as I must repeat once again, the first principle of all action is leisure. Both are required, but leisure is better than occupation and is its end.

The most perfect
political community is
one in which the middle
class is in control, and
outnumbers both of the
other classes.

Persuasion is effected through the medium of the hearers, when they shall have been brought to a state of excitement under the influence of speech; for we do not, when influenced by pain or joy, or partiality or dislike, award our decisions in the same way; about which means of persuasion alone, I declare that the system-mongers of the present day busy themselves.

We ought to be able to persuade on opposite sides of a question; as also we ought in the case of arguing by syllogism: not that we should practice both, for it is not right to persuade to what is bad; but in order that the bearing of the case may not escape us, and that when another makes an unfair use of these reasonings, we may be able to solve them.

With the truth, all
given facts harmonize;
but with what is false,
the truth soon hits a
wrong note.

Since the branch of philosophy on which we are at present engaged differs from the others in not being a subject of merely intellectual interest — I mean we are not concerned to know what goodness essentially is, but how we are to become good men, for this alone gives the study its practical value — we must apply our minds to the solution of the problems of conduct.

Temperance and
bravery, then, are
ruined by excess
and deficiency,
but preserved
by the mean.

Governments which have a regard to the common interest are constituted in accordance with strict principles of justice, and are therefore true forms; but those which regard only the interest of the rulers are all defective and perverted forms, for they are despotic, whereas a state is a community of freemen.

The pleasures
arising from
thinking and
learning will
make us think and
learn all the more.

There are three
qualifications required
in those who have to fill
the highest offices, -

(1) first of all, loyalty
to the established
constitution;

(2) the greatest
administrative
capacity;

(3) virtue and justice of
the kind proper to each
form of government.

The Good of man is the active exercise of his soul's faculties in conformity with excellence or virtue. Moreover, this activity must occupy a complete lifetime; for one swallow does not make spring, nor does one fine day; and similarly, one day or brief period of happiness does not make a man supremely blessed and happy.

Man, when perfected,
is the best of animals,
but when separated
from law and justice,
he is the worst of all.

Between friends
there is no need for
justice, but people
who are just still
need the quality
of friendship; and
indeed friendliness
is considered to be
justice in the
fullest sense.

Those who educate
children well are
more to be honored
than parents, for
these only gave life,
those the art of
living well.

Even if we could
suppose the citizen
body to be virtuous,
without each of them
being so, yet the
latter would be
better, for in the
virtue of each the
virtue of all is
involved.

Music has a power of
forming the character,
and should therefore be
introduced into the
education of the young.

The seat of the soul
and the control of
voluntary movement
— in fact, of nervous
functions in general,
— are to be sought in
the heart. The brain
is an organ of minor
importance.

I call that law
universal, which is
conformable merely to
dictates of nature;
for there does exist
naturally an universal
sense of right and wrong,
which, in a certain
degree, all intuitively
divine, even should no
intercourse with each
other, nor any compact
have existed.

Error is multiform (for evil is a form of the unlimited, as in the old Pythagorean imagery, and good of the limited), whereas success is possible in one way only (which is why it is easy to fail and difficult to succeed – easy to miss the target and difficult to hit it); so this is another reason why excess and deficiency are a mark of vice, and observance of the mean a mark of virtue: Goodness is simple, badness is manifold.

Every man should be responsible to others, nor should any one be allowed to do just as he pleases; for where absolute freedom is allowed, there is nothing to restrain the evil which is inherent in every man.

Those who are not
angry at the things
they should be angry
at are thought to be
fools, and so are
those who are not
angry in the right
way, at the right
time, or with the
right persons.

All who have
meditated on the art
of governing mankind
have been convinced
that the fate of
empires depends
on the education
of youth.

Knowledge of the
fact differs from
knowledge of the
reason for the fact.

We should behave
to our friends
as we would wish
our friends
to behave
to us.

The knowledge of
the soul admittedly
contributes greatly to
the advance of truth in
general, and, above all,
to our understanding of
Nature, for the soul is in
some sense the principle
of animal life.

Those who excel in
virtue have the best
right of all to rebel,
but then they are of
all men the least
inclined to do so.

What the statesman
is most anxious to
produce is a certain
moral character in his
fellow citizens, namely
a disposition to virtue
and the performance of
virtuous actions.

The true friend of
the people should see
that they be not too
poor, for extreme
poverty lowers the
character of the
democracy.

In practical matters
the end is not mere
speculative knowledge
of what is to be done,
but rather the doing of
it. It is not enough to
know about Virtue,
then, but we must
endeavor to possess it,
and to use it, or to
take any other steps
that may make.

It is the active
exercise of our
faculties in
conformity with
virtue that causes
happiness, and the
opposite activities
its opposite.

Leisure of itself gives
pleasure and happiness
and enjoyment of life,
which are experienced,
not by the busy man, but
by those who have
leisure.

A right election can
only be made by those
who have knowledge

The moral virtues, then, are produced in us neither by nature nor against nature. Nature, indeed, prepares in us the ground for their reception, but their complete formation is the product of habit.

It will contribute towards one's object, who wishes to acquire a facility in the gaining of knowledge, to doubt judiciously.

But since there is but
one aim for the entire
state, it follows that
education must be one
and the same for all, and
that the responsibility
for it must be a public
one, not the private
affair which it now is,
each man looking after
his own children and
teaching them privately
whatever private
curriculum he thinks
they ought to study.

A state of the soul is
either (1) an emotion,
(2) a capacity, or
(3) a disposition;

virtue therefore must
be one of these three
things.

To seek for utility
everywhere is
entirely unsuited
to men that are
great-souled
and free.

9 798356 933103